The Butterfly with a Broken Wing

Written by John Greenlee
Illustrated by Keefe Chamberlain

ISBN-13:978-0-9772747-7-2

This is a true story…

One sunny day in late October, Jeannette and Mike, who lived in the Adirondack Mountains in upstate New York, went for a bike ride together.

Jeannette stopped to take off her jacket, and when she did, she saw a Monarch butterfly in the field. As she bent down for a closer look, she saw the butterfly was hurt. Its wing was broken! Jeannette poured out her water bottle and gently put the butterfly inside.

When Jeannette got back home, she fed the butterfly small bits of pear (from a tree in her yard), along with water mixed with honey (from her own beehive).

Together, Mike and Jeannette learned more about how to help injured butterflies. With a little glue and tiny pieces of cardboard, they made a splint just the right size for a butterfly wing.

A whole week went by. Jeannette and Mike were worried. Would the splint be too heavy? Would the cat try to get the butterfly? Even if it could fly again, now it was nearly winter. How could it ever catch up with the other butterflies that were already a long ways away?

But there was no need to worry, because the butterfly was healed! It began to fly all around the room.

Elizabeth (who knew a lot about butterflies) told Jeannette and Mike they should find someone heading south to help them. So they put the butterfly in a shoebox and drove to Scotty's Truck Stop. "Would any southbound drivers like to deliver a package for us?" they asked. Everyone in the restaurant looked down. They kept drinking their coffee.

The truck drivers were surprised when they found out what was in the shoebox! Then one man, who had come from Alabama, raised his hand. He was willing to drive the butterfly all the way from New York to Florida!

A few days went by. Mike and Jeannette wondered what had happened to the butterfly in the shoebox on the long trip south. Then the truck driver called from Florida. The driver told them that he and the butterfly had made it. He had opened the box and it had flown away.

It was already making its way to Mexico, along with millions of other Monarch butterflies, just as they do every year. Mike and Jeannette were very happy. And the butterfly was, too!

Did you know that the butterfly is a symbol for Jesus Christ? Many followers of Jesus think of Him when they see one fluttering by. Over two thousand years ago, Jesus Christ lived in a land called Israel. He taught His followers that they could become friends with God! Jesus also told them that even though people sometimes did what was wrong, and did not always do what was right, He would take all of their sins away by giving His life for them and dying on a cross.

But Jesus did not stay dead! He rose again on the third day after He was crucified. Butterflies are a reminder of His resurrection. When the time is right, a caterpillar makes a cocoon, and as it wriggles its way out, it is transformed into a beautiful butterfly.

Jesus coming out of the grave was like that! Just as the butterfly leaves behind an empty cocoon, so Jesus left behind His empty tomb. When the followers of Jesus saw that He had risen, they were very glad! They knew that they did not have to be afraid of death ever again, because one day they would live forever with Jesus in Heaven.

Butterflies can also be reminders of the wonderful change that happens to us when we decide to become followers of Jesus ourselves. Because Jesus resurrected, He can give us a new life right now! That means we can start every morning knowing we are friends with God. The Bible says, "Therefore, if anyone is in Christ, he is a new creature; the old things passed away; behold, new things have come!"

Even though we love Jesus and try to follow Him as best we can, sometimes what we do or say makes Him sad. There are still times when we have trouble doing what is right and not doing what is wrong. Jesus intends for us to soar high like the butterflies, but there are days when it seems as if our wings are broken. We might wonder, how we will ever get off the ground again?

The good news is that Jesus helps us even then! Nothing is too hard for Him. Jesus is able to mend our broken wings. He can send us on our way again like the happy butterflies He intended for us to be. So the next time you see a butterfly floating by, thank Jesus for making you a brand new creation!

The End

Made in the USA
Monee, IL
15 May 2022

96455626R00017